Fire Station Number 4

THE DAILY LIFE OF FIREFIGHTERS

Fire Station Number 4

THE DAILY LIFE OF FIREFIGHTERS

BY MARY T. FORTNEY
PHOTOGRAPHS BY NORBERT VON DER GROEBEN

CAROLRHODA BOOKS, INC./MINNEAPOLIS

To Gary, Jimmy, and John, who explained their jobs to me with patience and humor, and to Norbert, who came up with the idea for the book. Thanks so much. —M. T. F.

To all the Livermore-Pleasanton Fire Department firefighters, especially Gary, John, and Jimmy—without their understanding and patience this book would never have happened. Thanks also to Mary Fortney for writing the text and to Ellen M. Banner for planting the seed for the book. And thanks to my mother, Alexandra, who always thinks my ideas are wonderful, even if they are crazy. —N. V. G.

Carolrhoda Books, Inc., c/o The Lerner Publishing Group
241 First Avenue North, Minneapolis, MN 55401 U.S.A.

Website address: www.lernerbooks.com

LIBRARY OF CONGRESS CATALOGING-IN-PUBLICATION DATA

Fortney, Mary T.
   Fire Station Number 4 : the daily life of firefighters / by Mary T. Fortney ; photographs by Norbert von der Groeben.
     p. cm.
   Includes index.
   Summary: Describes the various activities performed every day by fire fighters in Livermore, California, a suburb of San Francisco.
   ISBN 1-57505-089-7 (alk. paper)
   1. Fire extinction—Juvenile literature. 2. Fire stations—Juvenile literature. [1. Fire extinction. 2. Fire departments. 3. Fire fighters. 4. Occupations.] I. von der Groeben, Norbert, ill. II. Title.
TH9148.F67   1998
363.37'023—dc21   97-25891

Manufactured in the United States of America
1 2 3 4 5 6 – JR – 03 02 01 00 99 98

Contents

Introduction

You've probably seen firefighters speeding by in a fire engine, sirens wailing. Most people know that firefighters put out fires. But is that what they do all day?

Jimmy, John, and Gary work for the Livermore Fire Department in California.

Gary Rose, Jimmy McCraw, and John Moyles are firefighters. They work at Fire Station Number 4 in the California town of Livermore, a suburb of San Francisco with 65,000 people. Fighting fires is a big part of their jobs, but they don't fight fires all day long. There may not even be a fire every day. Still, Gary, Jimmy, and John have plenty to keep them busy.

Left: *Some firefighters slide down a pole to reach their fire engine below. Station Number 4 doesn't have a pole—it's a one-story building.*

Below: *Gary cools off with a cup of water after fighting a house fire.*

Station Number 4

Fire Station Number 4 is one of five **fire stations** run by the Livermore Fire Department. Each station takes care of fires and other types of emergencies in its area of the city. The **fire department** includes all of a city's fire-fighting operations—the stations, the office staff, and the **dispatch center** (the place that receives 911 emergency calls).

Gary has worked as a firefighter for seventeen years, Jimmy for twenty-five years, and John for twenty-seven years. With so many years of experience, they know a lot about fighting fires.

Gary, Jimmy, and John each had his own special reason for wanting to become a firefighter, but they all wanted jobs helping people. Gary was also looking for work that was exciting. Jimmy joined the department because he found that working at a fire station was like being part of a family. John carried on a family tradition by becoming a firefighter. His father, a firefighter, was a hero to him. John remembers that the kids in school envied him for having a firefighter dad.

Above right: *John goes out on a call.*

Right: *Jimmy takes care of some chores at the station.*

Firefighters' days are different from those of most workers. They don't go to an office, factory, or store every day from 8:00 A.M. to 5:00 P.M. The Livermore firefighters stay at the fire station for twenty-four hours at a time, from 8:00 A.M. one day until 8:00 A.M. the next day. Then they have twenty-four hours off before returning to work again. After two more twenty-four-hour shifts, with twenty-four hours off in between, they have four days off in a row. Most fire stations in the United States follow the same type of schedule.

To become a firefighter at the Livermore Fire Department, a person must pass tests of his or her fire-fighting knowledge and physical ability. In order to take the tests, an applicant must be twenty-one years old or older, a high school graduate, and physically able to do the job. The Livermore department also recommends that applicants take a fire-fighting class at a community college before applying for a job.

Jimmy, an engineer, takes a look under Fire Engine Number 4.

Captain Gary keeps the station running smoothly.

Part of John's job as firefighter is to operate the hoses.

At Station Number 4, Gary, Jimmy, and John always work together. For each twenty-four-hour shift, a **captain,** an **engineer,** and a **firefighter** are on duty. Gary, the captain, is in charge. He is responsible for making sure the fire station operates properly. Part of his job is to keep track of the work schedule, making sure that the right people come to work each day. Jimmy, the engineer, keeps the fire engine in good condition. He also drives the fire engine when they go out on a call.

John, the firefighter, is in charge of the hoses—he sprays water on the fire. He also helps take care of the equipment and assists with medical emergencies. John is called a firefighter because that's the title of his job. But the term "firefighter" is also used for anyone who fights fires. So Gary and Jimmy are firefighters, too. All the firefighters pitch in to help control a blaze.

The person in charge of all the firefighters is the **fire chief.** When there's a big fire, the chief rushes to the blaze to organize and direct the fire-fighting operation.

In 1974, the first female firefighter in the United States was hired. Before that, only men worked as firefighters. More and more women are finding jobs with fire departments. In 1995, the first women joined the Livermore Fire Department. By 1997, there were 5 female firefighters in the department. But that's still only a small number of the department's 125 firefighters.

Women do the same jobs as male firefighters, and they meet the same requirements for getting hired. But whether a fire crew is made up of men or women, firefighters work as a team. No matter who does the work, fighting fires and making sure no one gets injured are the most important parts of the job.

Above: *Jane Moorhead and Sabine Imrie talk during graduation ceremonies at the Livermore Fire Academy, where new firefighters are trained.*

Left: *Jane sprays water onto a burning house.*

Morning

For Jimmy, John, and Gary, a typical day begins when they report to work at 8:00 A.M. First, they change into their uniforms—dark blue T-shirts and cotton pants. All their clothing has to be cotton, because cotton is slower to catch fire than synthetic fabrics like nylon.

After arriving for work each morning (below), *each firefighter pins on a name badge* (above), *which has a star for every five years of service.*

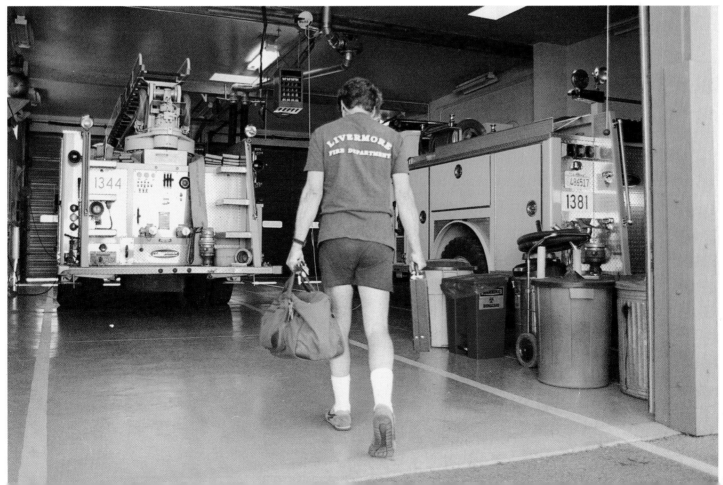

Jimmy has the first important duty of the day. He takes the fire engine out for a short ride, called a **pre-trip inspection.** He checks the brakes to be sure they are working and makes sure that the engine has enough water and oil. Jimmy also looks to see how much gasoline is in the tank. The firefighters keep the tank at least three-fourths full at all times, so they are always ready to rush out to a fire. Imagine what would happen if the fire engine ran out of gas on the way to a fire!

Jimmy climbs into the fire engine (above) *for the pre-trip inspection. Before taking the engine out for a ride each morning, he looks over the log book* (left).

The first part of the morning is exercise time. Fighting fires is a tough task. Firefighters must be strong, so they can hold the hoses steady when water shoots out with great force. Every year, the firefighters must pass a test to be sure they are physically fit.

Each fire station is equipped like a fitness center, with weight machines, stair-climbing machines, and stationary bikes. The crew exercises at or close to the station so they can always be ready to hurry out if an alarm sounds. Gary and John often walk around the block for their exercise—they usually go around nine times, which is equal to about three miles. Jimmy likes to work out by lifting weights.

John and Gary run laps around the Station Number 4 block (left). *Jimmy lifts weights* (below) *to keep his upper body strong.*

15

John mops the inside of the station.

The rest of the day—if they're at the station—is a mix of doing chores, eating, and relaxing. The firefighters also spend time studying. They keep learning about new techniques for fighting fires, and they review what they already know. If they're surrounded by flames, they don't want to stop and think, "What am I supposed to do now?"

At lunchtime, the three usually just make sandwiches. The firefighters have to shop for groceries, just as families do. But unlike families, Gary, John, and Jimmy drive to the supermarket in a fire engine. They can answer calls to the fire station on their radios—each crew member carries a radio. If there's a fire or medical call, they'll drop everything and respond.

No matter what the firefighters are doing—grocery shopping, sleeping, taking a shower, or talking on the phone—they are up and away if an alarm sounds. They can't afford to waste any time.

Firefighters go grocery shopping, too—Jimmy picks out broccoli for dinner (above). *Out in the parking lot* (left), *Jimmy opens the door for Gary and his bag of groceries.*

About one million firefighters in the United States work for free. These are **volunteer firefighters.** They don't get paid for fighting fires—they usually have other jobs. Most of the volunteer firefighters in the Unites States live in small towns that can't afford a fire department. A town will buy a fire engine, equipment, and an alarm system. When a fire alarm sounds, the volunteers come from wherever they are—a dinner table, a gas station, an office—and race to the fire.

Even though the Livermore department has paid firefighters, it has volunteer firefighters, too. Some volunteers work for free because they hope to become paid firefighters. Volunteering is a way to get experience. Jimmy got a job as a full-time firefighter after two years as a volunteer. Other volunteers don't want jobs as firefighters—they just want to help the community. Volunteer firefighters in Livermore are not allowed to go inside a building to fight a fire, but they can spray water from the outside. Volunteers also help the regular crews fight grass fires.

Above right: *Volunteer firefighters watch a house burn during a training exercise.*

Right: *Davina Flanagan, a Livermore volunteer firefighter, pulls hoses off the fire engine.*

Fighting Fires

Although Gary, John, and Jimmy do many different jobs, fighting fires is what they like best. Gary thinks putting out a fire is like a kid's game of fighting a dragon, except you're doing it as a team—and it's a life-or-death challenge. John says fighting fires is like being paid for playing cowboys. To Jimmy, fighting a fire is similar to a chess game—he enjoys the challenge of matching wits against the blaze. He also enjoys the fun of driving to a fire with the sirens sounding.

Even though Gary, John, and Jimmy may talk about fighting fires as a game, they know that it's a serious job. People's lives may be in danger, and their houses or businesses could be destroyed. That is why the firefighters dash out as fast as they can when an alarm sounds.

Firefighters enter a burning house.

Most people know that they should call 911 when a fire starts. In Livermore, all of the 911 emergency calls go to the dispatch center in the main police station. After the caller says whether it's a police, fire, or medical emergency, the **dispatcher** alerts whoever is needed. The dispatcher radios the fire station closest to the location of the emergency. At Station Number 4, the firefighters hear three beeps on their radios before a call comes in. Then the dispatcher gives them information about the call and its location. The dispatcher alerts more than one station if it's a big fire.

The firefighters can tell what size fire to ex-

At the Livermore Police Department's dispatch center, James Taylor (left) takes emergency calls and radios the fire stations as they are needed. John (above) receives a call on his radio.

Livermore firefighters put out a fire that started in an old trailer.

The firefighters can tell what size fire to expect by the number of alarms sounded by the dispatch center. One alarm is for a small fire. Two alarms are for a fire that's a bit bigger, such as a house fire. Most of the time, two fire engines and a fire truck race to one- or two-alarm fires. More than one station responds to fire alarms to make sure enough equipment is on hand to put out the fire. As the number of alarms increases, more equipment is sent to the fire.

This four-alarm fire started when someone tried to barbecue on the porch.

Three alarms are sounded for fires in stores or office buildings, or for smaller fires that have burned out of control. For a three-alarm fire, the Livermore Fire Department may even get help from fire departments in other cities. The highest number of alarms is six, for really big fires. The firefighters may work for up to ninety-six hours—four days—without resting when they are battling large, out-of-control fires. Forest fires, for example, may burn for days before being put out. When all the on-duty firefighters are out at a big fire, the Livermore Fire Department calls in off-duty firefighters to take over at the fire stations.

Gary on the roof at a house fire

Firefighters from Station Number 4 were sent to battle a six-alarm fire in Oakland, California, in 1991 and six-alarm wildfires in Southern California in 1996. The Oakland fire was the biggest fire on record in the San Francisco Bay Area—12,000 firefighters worked to contain the blaze. The fire was so hot that it melted the metal fire hydrants and the tires on the fire engines. At one point, John had to lie down on the curb so he could breathe cool air from the gutter. Hot air and the toxic gases produced by a fire rise, so the air closer to the ground is safer to breathe. When John teaches children about fire safety, he always tells them to escape from a fire by crawling along the floor.

Oakland, California, 1991

Whooooeeeeeooooo! Where would firefighters be without fire engines? All the fire engines and other vehicles used by firefighters are called **fire apparatus.** Fire engines are expensive—they cost between $200,000 and $500,000 each. You could buy fifteen to forty ordinary automobiles with that amount of money.

Fire Engine Number 4, also called "Tel-Squirt," is the engine at Station 4. It carries a fifty-five-foot ladder and is equipped to pump water from its three-hundred-gallon water tank or from fire hydrants. Besides the long ladder, Tel-Squirt has smaller ladders—one for use in attics, one for use on roofs, and a twenty-four-foot extension ladder that the firefighters use to climb up to a roof. The engine is equipped with wire cutters to cut electric wires, an ax to chop down walls, and some small fire extinguishers. It also has "jaws of life," which are used to get trapped people out of wrecked cars.

Right and above: *Fire Engine Number 4*

Livermore's fire apparatus used to be yellow because it was thought that yellow was easier to see at night. But the department decided that the color doesn't make much of a difference. They are repainting their vehicles red—the traditional color for fire engines. The Livermore Fire Department's fire truck (left) is red.

The only other vehicle at Station Number 4 is a small pickup truck with a water pump. This truck is called Patrol Number 4, and it's used for grass fires.

The Livermore Fire Department has a **fire truck,** which is kept at another station. This type of truck used to be called a hook and ladder truck. In order for a vehicle to officially be called a fire truck, it must carry 167 feet of ladder. The fire truck is used when fighting fires in tall buildings. Most people don't know the difference between a fire truck and a smaller fire engine, so they call them all fire trucks.

Some fire departments have salvage trucks that are used to clean up what's left of a building after a fire. A fire department may also have a rescue truck that firefighters use to help injured victims. The Livermore Fire Department is too small to afford these vehicles.

Firefighting equipment on Fire Engine Number 4

Fighting fires is hot, dirty, dangerous work, and the Station 4 crew needs special clothes and equipment to protect themselves from flames and smoke. Before Gary, Jimmy, and John rush to a fire, they put on **turnout clothes.** These fireproof and waterproof jackets and pants protect them from flames. Turnout clothes are yellow, which helps firefighters see each other more easily through the smoke.

Gary, John, and Jimmy wash their turnout clothes after a fire, because they get grimy from all the smoke and ashes. The firefighters have two sets of turnout clothes—they need to have a clean set ready if a fire alarm sounds before the first set is dry.

Dressed in turnout clothes, Gary is ready to answer a call.

Firefighters wear helmets made of leather for protection against falling pieces of burning wood or hot cinders. They also wear special leather gloves and boots. And they have masks to wear if the smoke and flames make it difficult to breathe. The masks are hung on the fire engine or kept right next to it, ready to be grabbed as the firefighters race off to a fire. Fire-fighting equipment must always be ready for the firefighters if an alarm sounds.

Above: *A firefighter's mask fits close to the face to prevent smoke from getting in. The mask is connected to an air pack on the firefighter's back.*

Left: *Jimmy rolls freshly washed turnout clothes out to dry.*

Livermore's fire truck at the fire training tower

Some of the fires that Gary, Jimmy, and John fight are practice fires. The Livermore Fire Department operates a five-acre **training center** where firefighters practice fighting fires. Fires are set inside the rooms of a six-story training tower made of concrete (which doesn't burn). Then firefighters work together to put the fires out. Firefighters also practice climbing the outside walls of the tower, like mountain climbers, in case they need to rescue someone from a tall building.

The firefighters also work on other skills at the training center. They practice rescuing people from a fire, dealing with medical emergencies, tying knots, and handling hoses and ladders.

Afternoon

If the firefighters aren't called away from the station, the day goes on as usual. After lunch, there are always chores to do. On Saturdays, the crew washes the fire engine. On Sundays, Gary, Jimmy, and John keep busy doing housework at the station.

Fire Engine Number 4 gets a bath.

The fire station is like home to Gary, Jimmy, and John, and they must keep it clean, just as families keep their homes clean. That means dusting, vacuuming, and emptying the trash. John takes care of most of the housecleaning. Gary is a good cook, so he fixes dinner for the crew. Jimmy likes to maintain the equipment used by the firefighters, and he keeps track of the tools in the station's workshop.

Jimmy washes the fire station windows (above). *Gary is the cook of the Station Number 4 crew* (left).

Since the three firefighters are at the station for twenty-four hours, they are on duty all day and night. They need some time to rest and relax. After they have taken care of chores, they watch television, read, or do whatever they want. Sometimes a sleepy firefighter will sneak in a quick nap. Often they sit and tell each other stories. John likes to ask Gary and Jimmy riddles that are printed on popsicle sticks.

Later, there's dinner to cook. Gary likes to keep the meals simple—spaghetti, barbecued chicken, salad. The three firefighters eat together at the kitchen table. John usually washes the dishes afterward.

Jimmy tells John a joke at the dinner table (above). *Gary likes to play darts when he has some free time at the station* (below).

More than Fighting Fires

Gary, Jimmy, and John can be called away from the fire station for many things besides fires. For starters, they answer medical calls if someone is hurt or having a heart attack. The dispatch center calls Station Number 4 when there are nearby medical emergencies. The dispatcher also calls the ambulance, but since there is only one in Livermore, it may be out on another call. The firefighters almost always arrive at the scene first.

Each fire crew includes a firefighter who is a **paramedic,** someone trained to handle emergency medical problems. Gary is the paramedic of the Station Number 4 crew.

Gary will check the patient's symptoms, decide what the problem is, and give the patient the necessary emergency treatment. Sometimes the firefighters can take care of the emergency, and an ambulance is not needed. But if the patient needs more care, the firefighters make sure the Livermore ambulance or one from a neighboring city arrives to take the patient to a hospital.

A medical call can be for something life threatening, like a heart attack or stroke, or for a less serious situation, such as an injury at a soccer game. But as with fires, the crew responds as quickly as possible. In the case of a heart attack, a person's brain is affected after only four minutes. Time four minutes on a watch, and you'll see that this is not a very long time!

Opposite page: Gary, the crew's paramedic, takes charge on a medical call. Paramedics must complete 1,200 hours of training in order to be qualified for the job.

Jimmy stands by Engine Number 4 on a call.

Sometimes the firefighters hurry out on a call, and it turns out to be a **false alarm.** Some false alarm calls are from people who see smoke coming from a barbecue and think a house is on fire. But people will occasionally call in a false alarm on purpose as a prank, which is a crime. The station gets fewer false alarms than it used to, because the caller's address flashes on the dispatcher's computer screen when 911 is called. This makes it easier to find the culprit.

False alarms can be dangerous—a traffic accident could be caused as the firefighters hurry out on an alarm. Also, the crew may have a harder time getting to a real emergency if they're busy with a false alarm.

One of the firefighters' jobs that is becoming more and more important is responding to **toxic spills.** A dangerous chemical may leak from a truck cruising down the highway, or dangerous chemicals may spill from a wrecked automobile. Sometimes toxic spills happen at factories or schools. Toxic spill calls come through the 911 emergency number. Gary, Jimmy, and John rush out just as they would for a fire, because toxic chemicals may be harmful to people. The Livermore Fire Department also has a special group called a "hazmat team" that is trained to work with hazardous materials.

When John, Gary, and Jimmy go out on toxic spill calls, they wear what they call "bunny suits." These suits cover the firefighters completely, but they have a clear, plastic window for the wearer to see out. They look a little bit like space suits. After the firefighters arrive at the toxic spill, they close off the spill area, called the **hot zone.** They also block traffic, so no one will get hurt.

Wearing "bunny suits," Gary and Jimmy take samples of a hazardous material.

The firefighters test the material to see what it is. But they don't clean up the spill. If it's on a highway, the California Highway Patrol is in charge of the cleanup. If it's on private property, the dispatcher calls a cleanup company certified by the state to do the job, but the owner of the property must pay for it.

The most common toxic spills are fuels, such as gasoline or diesel, because they are used in cars and trucks. The next most common are corrosive acids, such as battery acid or sulfuric acid. Sometimes the firefighters will get a call that a white powder has spilled on the highway. This could be a dangerous pesticide. As always, the firefighters hurry to the spot. Often they discover that the powder is a harmless substance, such as salt, sand, or cement. But they can't take a chance.

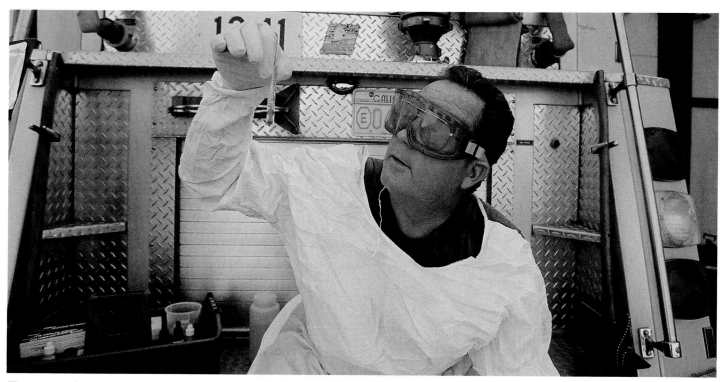

Toxic spills are dangerous not only to people—they can also harm animals and the environment. Jimmy runs some tests to find out what a spilled substance is.

Another of the firefighters' jobs is helping with **search and rescue missions.** They might search for a hiker lost in a nature preserve or use their equipment to rescue a motorist stuck in a car after an accident. As with other types of calls, the firefighters may be needed in the Livermore area or in neighboring cities. During the 1989 Loma Prieta earthquake in the San Francisco Bay Area, Gary, John, and Jimmy helped people trapped in the wreckage of a freeway. And during the 1996 floods in Napa Valley, they rescued people who were flooded out of their homes.

Some search and rescue missions involve looking for people trapped in burning buildings. John searches a smoke-filled room.

Jimmy and Gary inspect a business to be sure there isn't a gas leak.

The firefighters also handle service calls. On these types of calls, a child may be locked alone in a car. Or someone may have fallen on the street and need help. The firefighters do not rescue cats stuck up in trees, as they did in earlier days. But the Station Number 4 crew once had an unusual job after an earthquake. They helped a homeowner clean up after a three-hundred-gallon fish tank toppled, spilling water and fish all over.

There are some jobs that Jimmy, John, and Gary don't have to dash off to. Every year, the firefighters from the five Livermore fire stations grease and check all the fire hydrants in town to make sure they are working. They also inspect all businesses—restaurants, stores, factories, even doctors' offices—to make sure they have proper fire exits and enough fire extinguishers.

One job the firefighters especially enjoy is teaching fire safety to young people—from nursery schoolers to seniors in high school. In Livermore, a firefighter visits every class once a year to teach students what to do if they smell smoke or if their house catches on fire. This teaching pays off. One six-year-old boy from Livermore helped his family escape their burning house by using what he learned in a fire safety class.

John especially likes to teach the fire safety classes. He also makes sure his own children know about fire safety. Every time children come to visit his house, he puts them through a fire drill, too. One night at 4 A.M., in the middle of a rainstorm, John held a fire drill. The children were out of the house in 30 seconds. They each got a cup of hot cocoa as a reward.

John shows a young friend how to use a fire hose.

The Station Number 4 crew likes to join in community activities, such as this old-fashioned bucket drill between volunteer and professional firefighters.

When the firefighters are not busy with fires, emergency health calls, and inspections, they participate in community activities. If there's a fair or festival, the crew will be there, showing off their engine and telling the public about what they do.

Often, school groups come to the station for a tour. This is fun for the children, who get to sit in a fire engine. It's also fun for the firefighters, who love to visit with kids. But, as always, the firefighters must be ready to speed off to answer an alarm.

Nighttime

Bedtime for Gary, Jimmy, and John is about 9:30 or 10:00 P.M. Sometimes they study or read a bit before they go to sleep. They sleep in a dormitory with three fold-down beds. If they're lucky, no alarms come in, and they get a good night's sleep.

A quiet evening at Fire Station Number 4

But calls often come in during the night. That makes for a hard shift. One night the crew got to bed at 11:30 P.M., after answering a call at 10:00 P.M. Then they rushed out to answer alarms at 1:00, 3:00, and 5:00 A.M. They got very little sleep that night.

In the morning, Gary, Jimmy, and John are up and ready to turn the station over to the next crew by 8:00 A.M. Then they can go home to their families. After their time off, they're back, ready for another day on the job as a firefighter.

John pulls down his bed (above) *and studies for a while* (right) *before going to sleep.*

Davina (volunteer firefighter), John, Gary, and Jimmy, dressed in turnout gear, are ready for action.

For Gary, Jimmy, and John there is no typical day at Fire Station Number 4. They can be busy with fires, medical calls, or toxic spills. Or they can spend a slow day doing chores at the station. But one thing doesn't change—they are always on the edge, ready to answer an alarm at any time, day or night. That is the life of a firefighter.

Fire Safety

You can help the firefighters in your town by learning some fire safety tips. Many fires are started accidentally, and many people are hurt each year because they may not know the fire safety rules.

- Firefighters emphasize that every home should have smoke detectors because they save lives. Ask an adult to test your smoke detectors regularly to be sure they work.

- Talk to your family about how you would escape from each room of your house or apartment if there were a fire. Decide on a place—away from the building—where you would meet once you escaped. This way, you would know if everyone was safely out of the building. Practice your fire drill regularly, at different times of the day.

- Practice what you would say if you ever needed to call 911. You would need to tell the person who answers the phone what's happening. Then you would give your name and the address and telephone number of the place you are calling from. It's important to call the fire department quickly, but it's also important for you to be in a safe place. Get away from a dangerous fire first, then call 911 from the nearest phone.

- Don't play with matches, candles, cigarette lighters, or anything else that could start a fire. You can help by teaching younger children not to play with these materials.

- If you or someone you're with does accidentally start a fire, tell an adult right away. An adult might be upset with you for starting a fire, but he or she would be much more upset if you were hurt or if the fire got out of control. Be prepared to call 911 if the fire starts to spread.

- If a fire alarm sounds in a public building, look for the nearest exit and walk there calmly. Don't push or run. If someone falls, it would be harder for everyone to leave the building.

- Never use an elevator to escape a fire. Use the stairs. An elevator could stop at a floor where a fire is burning, or it could stop working and leave you trapped.

- If you ever need to escape a burning building, remember that hot, smoky air rises. Clean, cool air stays near the floor. *Crawl* to safety if you're in a smoky room.

- If you smell smoke or hear a fire alarm, feel a closed door before you open it. If the door is hot, don't open it. If there isn't another door or if you can't exit out a window, put towels or cloth (wet, if possible) around the cracks in the door. Stay close to the floor to avoid smoke, and stay calm. Stay by a window and open it just enough to get some fresh air and to call for help. If smoke starts to come in the open window, close it immediately.

- If your clothes catch on fire, *stop, drop,* and *roll. Stop* right where you are—running can make a fire worse. *Drop* onto the floor, then *roll* to put the fire out. Rolling on the ground cuts off the fire's supply of oxygen, making it go out.

- Once you're out of a burning building, never go back inside to rescue anyone or anything. This is the job of the firefighters—they know what they're doing.

Davina helps roll hoses back onto the fire engine.

Glossary

captain: the head of a fire crew, who makes sure the station runs properly

dispatch center: the fire department office that receives 911 calls about fires and other emergencies and decides which fire station or stations should respond

dispatcher: a person who works at the dispatch center and lets firefighters know where a fire, medical emergency, or toxic spill has happened

engineer: the member of the fire crew who drives the fire engine and keeps the vehicles in working order

false alarm: a situation in which a fire alarm sounds, but there is no fire

fire apparatus: vehicles used to fight fires, including fire engines and fire trucks

fire chief: the head of a fire department. The chief rushes to big fires in order to organize and direct the fighting of the blaze.

fire department: a city's fire-fighting operation, which includes fire stations, a dispatch center, and office staff

firefighter: the member of a fire crew who handles the fire hoses. Also a word for anyone whose job is fighting fires

fire station: a building that houses fire apparatus and firefighters

fire truck: the largest vehicle used by firefighters, which carries 167 feet of ladder

hot zone: the area where a potentially dangerous substance has been spilled

paramedic: a person trained to handle medical emergencies

pre-trip inspection: a trip that a fire crew member takes with a fire engine to be sure it's running properly

search and rescue missions: trips that firefighters make to look for and help people lost or in danger

toxic spills: accidental spills of dangerous chemicals, such as gasoline, diesel fuel, pesticides, and acids

training center: a place used to train crews in fire-fighting techniques

turnout clothes: fireproof and waterproof jackets and pants that firefighters wear to protect themselves from flames. Turnout clothes are usually yellow, a color that's easily seen in smoke.

volunteer firefighters: people who work without pay for a fire department

Index